CAREERS IN COMPUTER TECHNOLOGY™

CAREERS IN
Online
Gaming

Published in 2014 by The Rosen Publishing Group, Inc.
29 East 21st Street, New York, NY 10010

First Edition

Library of Congress Cataloging-in-Publication Data

Poolos, Jamie.
Careers in online gaming/J. Poolos.—1st ed.
    p. cm.—(Careers in computer technology)
Includes bibliographical references and index.
ISBN 978-1-4488-9592-2 (library binding)
1. Electronic games industry—Vocational guidance. 2. Computer games—Vocational guidance. 3. Electronic games industry. 4. Computer games.
I. Title.
HD9993.E452P66 2014
794.8023—dc23

                                                          2012040036

Manufactured in the United States of America

CPSIA Compliance Information: Batch #S13YA: For further information, contact Rosen Publishing, New York, New York, at 1-800-237-9932.

Contents

Are you ready for a career in one of the most fun and intense industries ever? Do you love video games? Are you really good at something? (It could be almost anything.) Then a career in online gaming may be just right for you.

What exactly is online gaming? An online game is in most ways like a PC or a console game. With many online games, the actual gameplay is identical to a typical console or PC game packaged in boxes and sold in retail stores. The main difference is in the way the games are distributed. While a conventional game is played on a local machine, an online game is played over the Internet or a mobile network on a PC, console, tablet, or mobile phone.

With online games, gameplay may involve multiple players in locations all around the world competing against one another or working in teams. It also includes single-player games distributed over the Internet or via cellular networks.

There are all kinds of games that are distributed online. Some, such as massively multiplayer online role-playing games (MMORPGs), can support hundreds or thousands of people playing the game over the Internet simultaneously. On the other hand, in social mobile gaming, gameplay is lighthearted and targeted toward casual gamers. In their excellent book *Fundamentals of Game Design*, Ernest Adams and Andrew Rollings say, "Online gaming is a technology rather than a genre, a mechanism for connecting players together rather than a particular pattern of gameplay."

The Finnish game developer Rovio sold more than twelve million copies of the online game Angry Birds.

But does a career in online gaming make sense? We all know how important it is to choose a career in an industry that is healthy and has opportunity for growth. So how healthy is the video game industry and online gaming now, and what will it look like in the future? According to a report from DFC Intelligence, the video game industry is doing $67 billion in business annually worldwide. That's a lot of power-ups. It's true that these days the video game industry is outperforming the overall economy. And in some cases, it's outperforming other high-stakes entertainment industries, such as the Hollywood film industry. Video games are wildly popular, and online games are a big part of this popularity. This is great news for young people considering careers in the industry.

We know how popular video games are now. But what about five or ten years from now? Will consumers still want to buy games? The good news is that according to the same report, the video game industry is forecasted to grow to $82 billion globally in the next few years. Compared to almost any other industry, that is a lot of growth over a relatively short period of time, making the computer game industry one of the most secure fields available. But the largest driver in this projected growth is online gaming, accounting for $35 billion of the overall $82 billion. This figure is up from $19 billion currently. In the next few years, according to *Forbes* magazine, "39 percent of console game revenue will be via online distribution and online revenue sources." By all indications, a career in online gaming is a smart choice from an economic perspective.

So it's a thriving industry, and online gaming is on the uptick. But where do young people fit in? There are many jobs in the computer game industry, and new jobs are being created every year. They require unique skill sets, just like any job in any other industry. But jobs in online gaming demand more than a high skill level: they require personality, the ability to have fun while working hard, and a sublime passion for making games.

Online gaming originated at the dawn of computer networking. In other words, as soon as people were able to connect computers, they began to play games on them. In 1972, the personal computer had yet to be invented. Big universities utilized central mainframe computers, with terminals scattered across their campuses.

The first online game is thought to have been developed for such a computer at the University of Illinois, with players at different terminals interacting with one another. A few years later, Multi-User Dungeon (MUD) games became all the rage. These were free, text-based, real-time fantasy games in which players typed messages to one another to direct gameplay. While MUD games were popular among the computer crowd, online games didn't reach a mainstream audience until 1993, when the game *Doom* was launched. *Doom* was a graphical first-person shooter that allowed a player to join multiplayer games over a network or to set the modem to direct dial friends to play.

As graphics became richer and worlds became more complex, online games demanded faster network services to support the heavy processing loads. The developers of *Quake* made a significant leap in online gaming when they developed a technology that made it possible for many players to engage in a 3-D world without server slowdown. This young technology was refined in 1997 with the release of *Ultima Online*, and online gaming was catapulted into the mainstream. Today, popular massively multiplayer online role-playing games like *World of Warcraft* and *Guild Wars* offer gamers some of the richest graphics and gameplay of all computer games. First-person shooter games such as *Halo* and *Counter-Strike: Global Offensive* bring players from all over the world together in action-packed gameplay.

Ubisoft's popular Splinter Cell Blacklist *has licensing tie-ins to military thriller novelist Tom Clancy. It is a first-person shooter in which multiple players compete with one another online.*

MOBILE GAMING

As the massively multiplayer games began to increase in popularity, a new kind of online game was just getting started. In 1997, the Finnish company Nokia, the world's leading mobile phone supplier, packaged a simple maze game called *Snake* as a standard feature on its phones. While packaging primitive games on phones became a popular practice, it wasn't until a few years later when phones began to support the Java programming language that developers and businesspeople began to see the potential of a mobile game market. Over the next ten years, development picked up, but it was slow because mobile phone manufacturers could not standardize the game-specific capabilities across the industry.

Apple's iPhone changed that with its advanced hardware, App Store, and open development process. The device itself allowed for higher-quality games compared to other phones. The App Store was revolutionary in the game industry because it allowed developers easy access to consumers. Compared to console and PC games, mobile games are much simpler, so they are less expensive to develop. New developers were attracted to the low development costs and direct access to consumers through the App Store, and mobile gaming took off.

THE MOST POPULAR MMORPGS

Massively multiplayer online role-playing games can support millions of subscribers whose avatars, or characters, play together over the Internet. These games are extremely popular among hardcore gamers.

GAME	PUBLISHER
WORLD OF WARCRAFT	BLIZZARD
GUILD WARS	NCSOFT
STAR WARS: THE OLD REPUBLIC	BIOWARE
MABINOGI II: ARENA	NEXON
ASTA: THE WAR OF TEARS AND WIND	POLYGON GAMES
THE WAR Z	ARKTOS ENTERTAINMENT
RAIDERZ	PERFECT WORLD ENTERTAINMENT
LUNA ONLINE	GPOTATO
MAPLESTORY	WIZET
ASSASSIN'S CREED 3	UBISOFT

Apple made it even easier for developers with the iPhone Developer Program, which offers standards and guidelines for iPhone apps. Since the App Store launched, more than twenty-five billion apps have been downloaded. Other manufacturers followed Apple's business model, including Google's Android operating system, which launched its own version of the App Store. Mobile games are so popular that more than 46 percent of teens play games on their mobile devices, according to the Pew Internet & American Life Project. With traditional game publishers joining the fray, along with major companies such as Disney and Viacom making games, and the scores of new companies sprouting up, the future of mobile game development is promising.

SOCIAL GAMING

Meanwhile, another competitor came along to soak up a share of the gaming audience. But it wasn't another game or genre; it was social networking. These online services and sites encourage the building of expanding social networks through communicating and sharing. Companies such as Myspace, Friendster, and later Facebook and Twitter created online environments that enticed portions of the gaming community away from games. Game developers, wanting to regain this audience, began to see a potential in social networking as a delivery device for their products. Developers quickly dove in to build lightweight games that weren't as serious as traditional games and were designed to appeal to casual gamers. These games are typically played on browsers or on mobile devices.

As social networking giant Facebook grew to prominence, unknown companies began to distribute games via online invitations. Zynga's *FarmVille* became one of the most popular social games in history, with more than one hundred million players. Players become engaged in affecting the outcome of the game as they care for virtual farms and interacted with other players to trade resources such as seeds and feed and to receive rewards. The company developed other popular games, including *Mafia Wars*, a competitor to another Facebook game, Kabam's *The Godfather*. The growth of social gaming has slowed but is gaining ground, expecting to hit more than $8 billion in revenues, according to the Casual Games Association.

SIMILARITIES IN THE DEVELOPMENT OF ONLINE GAMES

The development of online games is similar in most ways to the development of other games, and the careers are similar, too. The most significant difference is the computer languages with which browser-based games and mobile games are developed. While the multiplayer online games, console games, and PC games are created with sophisticated languages such as C++, mobile and browser-based games are typically written in Adobe Flash, PHP, or JavaScript. They are also simpler to author than complex games for powerful processors.

A second difference is in the engines on which these types of games are developed. Massively multiplayer online role-playing games require the most sophisticated engines in all of gaming. Although there are several of these engines in play today, the standard is the Unreal engine, which revolutionized online games with its ability to render detailed facial expressions and complex mechanics. In contrast, mobile and social games must be built with simple engines designed

Most online game developers require that new hires have at least a bachelor's degree. Candidates with advanced degrees in computer science, engineering, or art are highly desired.

specifically for the relatively small processors of phones, tablets, and browsers. Some of the engines commonly used in mobile gaming are Corona, Cocos2D, and Marmalade. A third notable difference is the maturity and rate of development of the technologies. Mobile and browser game platforms are still being improved upon by leaps and bounds. In online gaming, the technology never sleeps. So workers in online gaming should always be prepared to learn new technologies in this rapidly evolving industry.

CHAPTER ②
Game Designer

An online game designer has the central role in the entire game-making process. Game designers manage the central idea of the game and everything it involves, including plot, theme, characters, rules, and the gameplay experience. Game designers can specialize in any of a number of areas. No matter what his or her specialty, a game designer is often the most creative and visionary member of the team.

DUTIES

A game designer's primary duties can range from running team meetings to drawing storyboards and writing character dialogue. It's a real challenge to juggle the different kinds of work—the tasks that require the management of creative people and those that require deep, creative thinking in solitude. Game designers carry a lot of weight on their shoulders. The entire success of a game depends on their ability to deliver their vision in a compelling product.

Online game designers spend a good deal of their time on the creative side, dreaming up the core game features, such as story lines, role play rules, and character profiles. They have to be proficient at documenting and expressing their ideas so that the rest of the team can get on the same page. This documentation can include prototype mockups of gameplay screens and navigation menus, sketches of worlds, and storyboards that show the gameplay progression. Game designers also generate and document plotlines for certain kinds of games, and they design characters, including their backstories.

Some games require the game designer to generate missions and problems, and he or she must sequence them into a logical arrangement. Puzzle games such as *Curiosity: What's Inside the Cube*, made by 22 Cans, require novel design concepts dedicated to an intriguing central theme. This arrangement should strike a delicate balance that challenges the player as he or she progresses through the game. Yet, the challenge shouldn't be so difficult that the player gives up. All of these elements add up to the gameplay experience, which the game designer must manage throughout the entire development process.

Once the game takes shape, game designers spend a lot of time tuning the gameplay and fixing bugs. In an interview with *Game Career Guide*, game designer Ben Schneider sums up the process: "When we're closer to finished [with a game], everything boils down to testing, polishing, and tweaking." This is an important, ongoing part of the process of game making, and the game designer has to be adaptive to changes in the direction in which the game is moving as it is developed, as well as changes in timelines.

WHERE ARE THE JOBS?

According to the Entertainment Software Association (ESA), five states have the majority of video game employees.

A graphic artist works from a sketchbook to render rich three-dimensional characters in a fantasy world for a massively multiplayer online role-playing game.

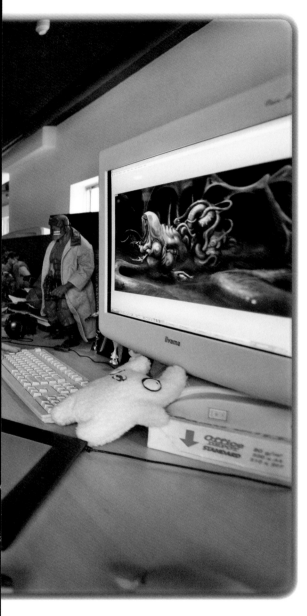

California is home to the largest number of video game workers in the country, with 41 percent of the total industry employees nationwide. Texas has the second-highest number of employees in the video game industry, with 13,613 workers. Washington has the third-highest number of employees, with 11,225 workers. New York has the fourth-highest number of employees, with 5,474 workers. Massachusetts has the fifth-highest number of employees, with 4,692 workers.

Recently, many states have passed laws to incentivize the video game industry to do business locally, including Pennsylvania, Georgia, North Carolina, Florida, and Louisiana, to name a few. It's reasonable to think that jobs in the computer game industry, especially in online gaming, will be available in many cities across the country.

EDUCATION REQUIREMENTS

As a group, video game designers are one of the best and most broadly educated of all employees in the game industry. They can have diverse backgrounds that help them understand the various disciplines that feed a game design, such as the flow of standard story lines, history, game strategy, behavioral psychology, and sports. In fact, the game designer has to know the basics of how to do all the other tasks and jobs described in this book and the impact of each on the game.

With that in mind, it's important to understand that not very many people begin their careers as game designers. Most start in testing and quality assurance, art, or programming. Many hold more than one of these positions before they become game designers.

HIGH SCHOOL

A high school student who aims to become a game designer must prepare for college coursework. That means taking advanced math and science courses. Most university and technical programs that cater to game design require that applicants demonstrate passion and proficiency in writing and design. In most cases, applicants must have completed advanced mathematics coursework in high school and have a strong foundation in the sciences as well, particularly physics. Art courses help students develop the fundamentals of design, color, and other concepts. These skills are necessary for game designers whose main focus is on the artistic elements of a game.

Many school districts offer students the option of attending technical and vocational schools. Technical high schools provide curricula that focus on a profession. A technical school program typically offers courses in the basic subjects necessary for admission to a university or college. These can be good options for students who don't excel as students in traditional academic environments.

It's also important to know the market. That means playing a lot of video games with the goal of understanding the logic behind the design. Students should join or start gaming clubs and computer programming clubs.

POSTSECONDARY EDUCATION

College is pretty much mandatory for a game designer. Gone are the days when an enthusiastic game player with above-average analytical skills and a few programming courses under his or her belt could waltz into a game studio and sell executives on his or her abilities. Now a candidate must have a bachelor's or master's degree just to get in the door. Game designers who have completed only an associate's degree cannot expect to move beyond an entry-level position without further education and training.

More universities now have programs that are geared specifically to game design. Often these courses are offered within computer science or media departments. They can include game prototyping, level design, video design, art and animation, and other skills like project management.

One school that offers a bachelor of science degree in game design is DigiPen Institute of Technology. According

A student programs a video game at a Tech Savvy for Girls Camp held at Pennsylvania State University.

to its course description, the program combines coursework in computer science with humanities, business courses, social sciences, and the fundamentals of art. Students learn core languages such as C and C++, scripting languages, and database technology and tools.

With an eye toward reflecting the work environment in the gaming industry, most classes focus on projects created by teams of students. According to DigiPen's course description, "Students in the Bachelor of Science in Game Design program design, prototype and iterate their projects in a collaborative, deadline-driven environment, helping them

INTERVIEW WITH RAFAEL J. BROWN, CREATIVE DIRECTOR AT GLASS LAB

Describe your job in five words.

Rafael J. Brown: Designing fun worlds and games.

What was the first game you ever played?

RJB: *Pac-Man.*

At what age did you first realize making games was what you wanted to do?

RJB: Twenty-five. I'd been making games since I was seven. I just didn't realize that it could be a career until I was twenty-five.

What did you do in school to prepare for your job now?

RJB: In high school, I took a wide workload of honors and AP courses. I was the founder and head of multiple clubs, I did team sports each season, and I was involved in a school initiative to revise the curriculum to be more inclusive of other cultures. In college, I took courses in psychology, art, computer science, history, architecture, film, creative writing, as well as lots of other areas (biology, chemistry, political science, etc). Having a well-rounded liberal arts education is absolutely essential because you have to be able to draw skills from a wide range of fields to make games and draw inspirations for your games from a wide range of aspects of real life.

What is the most rewarding aspect of your job?

RJB: Getting to the point in development where the game is appearing before you, and realizing that while it came from your creative vision, the game can still surprise you. The best games are creatively engaging and surprising because they start from personal ideas and are then built collaboratively by your team.

What is the coolest aspect of gaming in education right now?

RJB: Putting tools of creative expression in the hands of students and teachers. There is a growing movement of game developers like myself that want to bring fun, interactivity, and immersion to education. Games are great tools that teachers can use if we only help shape games for education. We recognize that games have a tremendous amount of learning embedded in them and that students are way ahead of teachers and parents in understanding the power of games. We need to harness student energy and creativity and show teachers and parents that games can contribute to education in meaningful ways.

What is the future of gaming in education?

RJB: Making games that don't feel like homework and making games where students can create and learn through doing and creating. The future of gaming in education is teachers able to go online and search for games that provide specific elements of curriculum. They should be able to select them and introduce them into the classroom. Parents and teachers should be assured that these games have educational content and structured learning that can be assessed and validated. Students should be able to enjoy games that are fun and engaging and have deeply immersive experiences.

develop the communication and team skills necessary to succeed in a real-world setting."

The latest thinking on postsecondary programs that focus on game design supports the idea that hands-on experience is a big part of a successful candidate's training. Taking an idea to concept and then making it into a product is a complicated task, and real-world game makers move at warp speed. Students gaining experience within the protective, instruction-oriented environment of a learning institution have more freedom to learn at a beginner's pace as they are exposed to the ins and outs of working within a development team.

However, it's important to remember that these programs are relatively new. Even accounting for the recent growth of game design bachelor's and master's degree programs at reputable colleges and universities, almost all game designers today have college degrees. They tend to be in computer science or in a multidisciplinary field. These fields combine computer science with liberal arts. In an interview with Web site videojug, Harry Ravenswood, lead game designer at the British game maker Kuju, calls the position of game designer a "nameless creative job, sometimes having many technical and creative jobs." Like many industry veterans, Ravenswood says that as the universities grow their game-specific majors to fit the game industry's needs, graduates of those programs will be more successful as game designers.

Yet for now, Ravenswood says a broad qualification is probably going to be very useful. "I'd be wary of anyone who had done nothing but game design as a course [in education]." He suggests students mix science, such as chemistry and physics, with traditional liberal arts courses. "I think the gist of game design is a good technical base. Sciences will do that for you," Ravenswood adds. "Learn to write well, and a good way to get that is through art history and English literature."

CHAPTER 3

Artist and Animator

In the context of computer games, "artist" is a blanket term that includes multimedia artists and animators—the people who create the environments, characters, and objects in a game and determine how they move. Essentially, an artist designs a game's visual style using methods such as drawing, motion capture, and 3-D modeling.

DUTIES

An artist's job is to start with a game designer's basic ideas and use his or her vision to develop concepts, or prototypes. These concepts are then taken through iterations that involve review by other members of the creative team, incorporating the feedback the reviews generate, and reviewing again until the team (or the boss) is satisfied with the visual quality of the game.

Anyone who plays games has noticed the improvement in the quality of art and animation from one online game to the next. A big-budget online game such as *World of Warcraft* often utilizes rich, elaborate settings called virtual worlds. These games also include characters and costumes rendered in great detail. This kind of art is striking, but it's expensive, meaning it requires a lot of computer data, or bandwidth, to process. In contrast, the art in a mobile online game such as *Angry Birds* is much simpler and often cartoonish in order not to overload the processors on mobile devices.

The industry has room for artists with different tastes and talents. There are a number of jobs that artists can have:

- Art director: Coordinates with lead development team, manages artists, budgets and schedules, works with game designers and others to define the game's aesthetic qualities.
- Lead artist: Manages a team of artists. If there is more than one team of artists working on the game, he or she may manage all the teams. Plans and distributes work to artists, and makes sure all art meets the standards and vision of the art director.
- Concept artist: Translates the visions of designers and other artists into concepts. Concepts can include landscapes, characters, and objects.
- Modeler: Builds 3-D characters and environments based on concept art. Sometimes modeling involves digitally painting and wrapping 2-D textures on a digital frame. Sometimes it involves creating skeletons that animators control.
- Animator: Makes models move. Models can be characters or objects in the game. The animator digitally controls the movements of the model, such as character movements, object movements, and landscape movements.

EDUCATION REQUIREMENTS

Although formal education is not always necessary, most developers prefer candidates who have received

Professor Joseph Saulter, cofounder of the Urban Video Game Institute, demonstrates 3-D animation software at an Atlanta, Georgia, college summer workshop.

foundational instruction in art, graphic design, game design, or a related area. Many game artists have a bachelor's degree from a university or college or a degree from a technical school that features a program that specializes in game art and animation. Artists with senior positions often have master's degrees.

Artists in the gaming industry must have a strong background in art theory and be familiar with classical and contemporary art styles and methods of creating that art. They must master traditional techniques, such as form, line, color, and composition. They must also know how to use the latest tools, like modeling and animation software.

HIGH SCHOOL

The best advice for high school students who are considering careers as artists and animators is to spend as much time as possible creating art and learning about how computers work. Students should take as many art classes as possible, especially classes that focus on drawing the human form. Art clubs, computer programming clubs, and gaming clubs can be beneficial as well. Even a job selling video games will give a student an opportunity to learn about the computer industry at the retail level.

Students should take every available advanced computer course and high-level math course. The knowledge a student gains in these courses is valuable in positioning him or her for succeeding in ongoing postsecondary courses and later in a career. The idea is to connect the disciplines of art, computer science, and mathematics in the context of gaming.

THE MOST POPULAR MOBILE GAMES

As the popularity of gaming grows, publishers become more brave about producing different types of games. These are some of the most popular mobile games today.

GAME	PUBLISHER	GENRE
MIRROR'S EDGE	ELECTRONIC ARTS	ADVENTURE
KELIME AVI	FUGO	BOARD
SUBWAY SURFERS	KILOO APS	ACTION
ASSASSIN'S CREED	GAMELOFT	ROLE-PLAYING
TEMPLE RUN	IMANGI STUDIOS	ACTION
EVE OF THE GENESIS	KEMCO	ROLE-PLAYING
RAGE OF BAHAMUT	MOBAGE, INC	FANTASY ONLINE ROLE-PLAYING
BOGGLE	EA MOBILE	BOARD
CURIOSITY: WHAT'S INSIDE THE CUBE?	22 CANS	MISCELLANEOUS

POSTSECONDARY

College-level art training for artists and animators includes courses in illustration, 3-D modeling and animation, color theory, interface design, and scene design. Candidates for jobs as game artists must be proficient in the tools of the trade before an employer will consider hiring them. These may include basic imaging software, such as Adobe Photoshop, Illustrator and Flash, as well as ActionScript

Adobe Photoshop has long been the graphic artist's tool of choice for developing textures for models, terrain, and environments when creating worlds in complex online games.

and FLEX. However, the tools the professionals use are constantly evolving, and it's important that artists in the game industry stay current with the latest software.

Postsecondary education programs that combine aspects of art theory with practical training are a good choice. For many students, programs that offer hands-on instruction yield the best results. Students work in teams to learn what real-world art and animation at a game studio is like. Excellent programs are available at art institutes and art-oriented trade schools and in traditional colleges and universities.

Programs such as the one at the Art Institute of Pittsburgh offer instruction in manual and computer-based

A professor at Shawnee State University prepares a lesson in 3-D modeling at the university's gaming department.

artistic skills and 3-D modeling and animation. Students then move to intermediate courses in character and object animation and design and lighting. As they progress to advanced courses, students learn more about the game production process, including project management and level design. Throughout the program, students develop skills and experience that come with working in teams. By the end of the program, each student will have produced a professional-quality portfolio that demonstrates drawing and design abilities. Students use their portfolio to showcase their work to prospective employers.

Another route is the traditional bachelor's degree. The major could be in almost anything: humanities, art, design, engineering, etc. The student must then generate a portfolio of work that demonstrates his or her skills. Since programs specifically for game art are relatively new, most artists in the game industry are graduates of traditional colleges. This is a great option for the individual who is motivated to excel in academics and to make an effort outside of the classroom to learn about game design, art and animation tools, and art theory.

CHAPTER 4

Producer

The producer's role isn't easy to define because there are many different variations, depending on the publisher and the studio. However, across the video game industry, producers are responsible for both leading and supporting the project. One way to think about the role: producers are less involved in actually making a part of the game themselves as they are in enabling others to make the game. Their job is to problem-solve and remove obstacles from the paths of developers and other members of the team.

The role requires an understanding of traditional online game development and mobile online game development, and how the various teams work with one another to create a game. For example, traditional online games such as CCP's *Eve* are developed over long time periods, up to a few years, by large teams with flexible project schedules. At the other end of the spectrum, lightweight social games such as Disney's *Wreck It Ralph* are typically developed over much shorter time periods by far fewer people working in parallel with one another. In addition to a knowledge of game development methodologies, the position also requires outstanding management and communication skills.

Producers are in charge of delivering the game on time and on budget. It's a lot of responsibility, but it's a great career for those who want to lead.

DUTIES

Producers are the "bosses" of the entire team—or at least they act like they are. Each serves as the chief organizer of his or her entire product and ensures that everything that needs to get done gets done. They are responsible to the publisher or executives to deliver the game on time and on budget. This means they have to manage the great ideas of a lot of creative people on the development team and make the tough decisions about which ideas can be realistically achieved by deadline and which need to be shelved or saved for a future release or update.

Producers are called on to manage all of the day-to-day operations of the teams, enabling communication between them, calling and organizing meetings, and solving problems. When they aren't working directly with their teams, they are keeping development costs on budget as well as keeping the teams on schedule with development.

Producers also act as the liaison between their development teams and the executives, sales teams, and marketing teams that represent the publisher's interests. When a problem arises, their job is to gather information from the appropriate personnel, weigh the risks, and make the top-level decisions about the best course of action. They must work with upper management, communicating the progress of development and any information that enables executives to make their decisions in regard to the business.

Finally, it is often the producer's job to represent the product and team to the publisher and to the media. This may involve doing interviews, presenting concepts at shows,

AN INTERVIEW WITH JEFF FENNEL

Name: Jeff Fennel

School: Butte College

Job Title: Instructor (3-D modeling/concept art and design/Photoshop)

Companies: Freelance; concept art and UI design for Zynga; art director/ game designer for Rainbow Studios; designer/artist for Monkey Business; other clients include 3DO, Sega, Sony, EA

How did teaching fit into your career plan?

JF: It just developed out of my interest in sharing. The first time I realized I liked it and was good at it, I was in college myself in graphic design. A high school kid came into the drafting store where I worked and asked if I could tutor him. He had the same drafting/architecture teacher I had in high school, so it was cool. Anyway, I really enjoyed it and made it a goal to one day teach. Also, and this is important, being an art director is basically the same thing as being a teacher or mentor, so it was a natural development.

Why would anyone want to teach?

JF: Well, if you're passionate about what you do, communicate well, and enjoy sharing your experience, it can be great.

What kind of person does well at a program like yours?

JF: Someone with a goal. Students who know where they're headed and what they want to get out of a program excel.

What does the program in which you teach offer? For example, only art/ animation, or does it extend to game design and programming?

JF: We just established a degree in applied computer graphics. We offer courses in concept art and design, 3-D modeling and animation, game theory, programming, and other related subjects. So yes, we're trying to put together a comprehensive game design and production program.

What are your students good at once they graduate the program?

JF: Understanding the process and how the pieces come together. They understand game theory, engineering, design, and art principles.

What advice do you have for high school students looking forward to careers in art and animation in gaming?

JF: The same advice I would have given myself...work hard, be curious, be aware, and do your best. Always. Research the top schools. See what it takes to get in them. Then do it.

Game developer Zynga revolutionized social gaming on Facebook and Google with its hit games Zynga Poker, FarmVille, YoVille, and ChefVille.

sitting on panels, and any number of other public-facing activities designed to promote the game or the company.

EDUCATION REQUIREMENTS

Producers should have excellent skills in scheduling, organization, communication, and leadership. Most of these skills are not developed in high school or college, but on the job. So most producers have worked their way up the ranks, often starting in quality assurance (QA) and later being promoted to an assistant or associate producer. Once an associate has proven that he or she can be trusted with managing multiple aspects of the game development process, he or she is eligible for promotion to producer.

HIGH SCHOOL

High school students considering jobs in production should think about their education trajectories, including the jobs where they plan to start. Considering the options mentioned in this section, the best advice is to pursue a course of study that puts the individual in the best position to be hired by a game developer. This will be a job the individual will be comfortable, stimulated, and happy working at for several years. He or she will gain experience and work toward the producer position. The course of study should accommodate this choice.

Because it is important to know the game industry and what makes one game better than the next, the student should be an avid gamer. Because management skills and

Criterion games

Matt Webster
Executive Producer

Criterion Games' Need for Speed: Most Wanted *is an open-world racing game in which multiple players can choose their own routes to the finish line in a virtual online world.*

experience are so important to the role, the student should take every available opportunity to take on leadership roles where he or she is managing a project or a team.

POSTSECONDARY

Unlike most jobs in computer gaming, the producer's role is not necessarily a technical one. However, since almost all producers start in another area of game development, many students interested in such a career prepare for initial positions as testers, programmers, engineers, or artists. Others get

ASK THE EXPERT: SEAN DUNN

Company: Impossible Studios/Epic Games

Job Title: Studio director

Years in the Game Industry: 23

Describe your job in five words.

Sean Dunn: Herding programmers, artists, and designers.

What was the first game you ever played?

SD: *Pong* or Atari 2600 *Combat.*

At what age did you first realize making games was what you wanted to do?

SD: Twenty-one. My professional baseball hopes had come to an end, and games were what I did second best.

What is the best part of your day?

SD: The moment I arrive at the studio and get to greet the most awesome set of game developers in the world.

What did you do, and/or what would you have done, in high school and in postsecondary school to prepare for your job now?

SD: While in high school, my father bought me a Commodore 64, and I tinkered with programming and played a ton of games. The programming helped me in college, where I got a computer science degree. The games I played steered me toward game development as a career. Having a computer science degree proved to be essential.

What is the most rewarding aspect of your job?

SD: Seeing an idea formed on paper, either in story form or from the hand of a concept artist transform over years into a finished product being played by millions of gamers around the world.

What is your favorite game genre and why?

SD: It used to be competitive FPS [first-person shooter] games, but I've recently become a serious MOBA [multiplayer online battle arena] addict.

I play way too much *League of Legends* now.

What would you have been had games not existed?

SD: I can't even begin to contemplate a world without games. I think I just would have been sad.

What is the coolest aspect of gaming in education right now?

SD: I love how games turn people onto things like math. One of my son's friends was talking about how much he hated math one day, then ten minutes later was talking about armor penetration values in an RTS [real-time strategy] and how they had a scaling effect on damage over time. When I pointed out that he had just solved an algebraic equation for fun, he thought that was pretty cool.

What is the future of gaming in education?

SD: I think gaming and technology are moving way too fast to try and predict this. I think that once educators realize games can be an avenue into the minds of kids instead of something that just prevents them from doing homework, we'll see much more innovation in educational games. There are so many things teachers can use from games to entice kids to learn. When you point out the art, writing, math, problem solving, economics, and social aspects of gaming, you can apply those areas of interest to grab kids' attention.

college degrees in business administration, where they develop the knowledge necessary to understand the basics of how a business runs, project management, and some basic legal concepts.

Part of developing scheduling and project management skills involves learning the tools of the trade. Producers are expert users of business applications such as Microsoft Word, Project,

A Ubisoft spokesperson introduces an Electronic Entertainment Expo audience to the highly anticipated open-world stealth game Assassin's Creed III.

Outlook, and Excel. It helps to learn C++, Assembly, Java, and Visual Basic in order to facilitate precise communication with technical team members like engineers and programmers.

Any prospective producer benefits from experience where he or she is responsible for supervising the work of others. Game companies want to see that the producer has learned to apply the skills he or she learned about in real-life situations.

INTERNSHIPS AND TRAINING PROGRAMS

In an interview conducted by Jill Duffy and published on the Web site Game Career Guide, Ellen Beeman, an executive game producer with more than fifteen years of experience in the industry at companies such as Microsoft, Monolith, Electronic Arts, Origin, and Disney, recommends to young would-be producers, "Look for opportunities prior to or outside of the game industry to build team leadership and creative direction skills." She says, "In college, I worked part-time at a music studio as a producer. It never amounted to much, but that managerial experience helped me get my first project director job at Sierra. Any professional experience, even not related to the game industry, is great. It all helps."

For students in game-specific programs, Beeman shares this more specific advice: "Students at game development colleges who are getting a degree in programming or art, but know they want to go into production, [should] look for opportunities to manage a small team."

CHAPTER 5

Gaming Software Engineer

Gaming software engineers are the architects of the game code. With their deep understanding of the capabilities of computer hardware, databases, and the programming languages used in game development, gaming software engineers determine how all of the many parts of the game design will come together in code.

Gaming software engineers for online games must have excellent organizational skills, communication skills, problem-solving abilities, analytical abilities, and high-level knowledge of the technologies used in gaming. This is a very technical job for individuals whose ability to understand high-level mathematics, systems integration, and continually developing technology is well above average.

DUTIES

Working hand-in-hand with the game designers, gaming software engineers begin with the game concept and plan out the best way to code the game. They determine the technologies that are necessary to accomplish the design goals and then figure out the best way to combine these technologies. The process may begin with a prototype and evolve over weeks and months as the team learns what works and what falls short.

Online gaming software engineers are required to write the technical design specification, essentially a timeline

ADVICE FROM DAVID LUOTO, CREATIVE DIRECTOR, EA PARTNERS, ELECTRONIC ARTS

"People want to give you advice on how to get into the game industry. I'm here to give you some reasons why you should get in. You might be thinking, 'I've got the only reason that matters. I really like games.' And yes, you're right. A passion for games is necessary. But is it enough?

"Questioning your love of games might sound a little crazy, but it happens all the time when you're making a game. You've been on a project for a couple years, working toward one deadline after another, and it's unclear if you're anywhere close to finding that 'magic' that will make the game. Maybe it's 2 AM, you're grumpy, and you stopped using the word 'fun' days ago. You've been looking at the same levels over and over and over. It's like you just watched a comedy film a hundred times and, guess what? None of the jokes are funny anymore. It's at a time like this that you reach down deep inside to reconnect with all the other reasons, outside of your passion for games, that attracted you to the game business. And here are a few:

"The people. Get your favorite game and take a look at the game credits. You might be surprised at the number of people it takes to make a game. That's because games are a hugely collaborative effort. It takes a lot of people to develop a game, test it, advertise it, and distribute it. And you need people with different skills, talents, and training. Consider it a huge fringe benefit that you get to work with a lot of sharp people, all with a variety of interesting passions and personalities. You'll make friends for life, and your life will be richer for it.

"You get paid to do this. There is something fun about saying that you make games for a living. I have great respect for people who do something just for the love of it. And doing something you hate just to pay the bills is a terrible compromise. But if you can get paid to do something you love, it's the best of all worlds.

HIGH SCHOOL

Mathematics is the foundation for engineering, and high school students who expect to be admitted to an excellent, or even reputable, bachelor's program in engineering or computer science must excel at the highest-level math courses their school offers. The same goes for computer courses.

Many high schools now have clubs whose members are interested in designing and building computer games and even smartphone applications. These clubs offer an excellent environment for learning from others, collaborating, and understanding engineering projects. Students can also hone their skills and demonstrate their abilities by creating their own independent demos, even simple ones like tic-tac-toe or hangman.

POSTSECONDARY

As a rule, a bachelor's degree in computer science or engineering, especially computer engineering, is required for a position as a gaming software engineer. Such a degree can provide the candidate with a solid background in the various languages used to make games and in the engineering concepts he or she will use on the job. Courses in computational mathematics, including vector algebra and algorithmic game theory, provide the framework for approaching the challenges that come with engineering complex software.

As upper-level courses in engineering are often project-based, students who wish to one day become lead software engineers should take every opportunity to volunteer to lead project teams or should assert themselves into roles as project organizers. Communication courses are useful as well.

Students enrolled in university video game programs have plenty of opportunities to share ideas with team members and pitch concepts to larger groups.

INTERNSHIPS AND TRAINING PROGRAMS

Students seeking software engineering positions can improve their chances by signing up as interns to get some experience. Many of the larger video game publishers and studios, such as Blizzard and Electronic Arts, offer internships every summer. These positions are usually highly competitive. While most studios really need experienced engineers, many have a policy of hiring interns in order to build long-term relationships with potential applicants.

Some colleges and universities have internship placement programs. For example, MIT's career services center

AN INTERVIEW WITH LISA CHING

Company: Kind of Strange Games, Real Life Plus

Job Title: Software contractor and principal engineer

Years in the Game Industry: 27

Describe your job in five words.

Lisa Ching: Designing*, programming, debugging, tech writing.

*As in how the code should provide functionality for a task, module, or system

What was the first game you ever played?

LC: The first computer game was a space war text game, but I can't remember the name. I think *Pac-Man* was my first arcade game. *Pong* was the first home console game.

At what age did you first realize making games was what you wanted to do?

LC: At eighteen, I was programming simple text games for fun while I had my first programming class (Fortran) in college, and continued programming games for fun afterward. However, I had never thought of programming games until my late twenties.

What is the best part of your day?

LC: I enjoy programming. I also think it's very cool to make video games that are fun for people to play. So it is great that I can be paid to program video games.

What did you do in school to prepare for your job now?

LC: Getting an electrical engineering degree was a great way to prepare. The engineering training emphasizes problem solving, which really helps for tricky software bugs, as well as lots of math background.

What is the most rewarding aspect of your job?

LC: Working with the game designers and the challenge of making the design come to life.

What is your favorite game genre and why?

LC: Currently MMORPG [massively multiplayer online role-playing game], as in *World of Warcraft*. I like the variety of game play–there is adventuring with your friends and exploring your world, leveling up your character, gearing up your character, the auction house game, the social aspects of being in a guild.

What is the coolest aspect of gaming right now?

LC: Having the Wii making video games far more accessible for non–hard-core gamers. I am impressed when I hear friends talking about their grandparents playing Wii games with the kids. When you have video games connecting with the whole family.

Technically speaking, the iPad game genre is coming up with some fun stuff; the challenge of working with more limited hardware is bringing out the more creative side for some companies.

What is the future of gaming?

LC: This new generation of kid seems very technically connected (e.g., texting, Facebook). Integrating the touch screen for serious games could be something new. I find that after using my iPad, when I go back to my computer, I am touching the screen sometimes when I want to interact with the display. I have heard that parents who let their young kids use their iPad also see those kids touching the computer monitors to attempt to interact with the computer.

uses MonsterTrak to help students gain experience, and sophomores may participate in the Undergraduate Practice Opportunities Program, where many find internships.

CHAPTER 6

Programmer

Game programmers are the members of the team who make the game designers' ideas come to life. They write the lines of code that tell the computer how to run the game, from the game's rules to how graphics display on the screen. In fact, they build the game line by line, using multiple coding languages, based on the kind of game and the platform.

The simplest online game may utilize several programmers, but most use several teams of programmers, each group working on a specific area of the game, such as coding the graphics engine. Some programmers specialize in tuning gameplay. Others may work on developing more efficient ways to optimize mobile delivery.

Game programmers need a deep understanding of computer languages, computational math, and gameplay. Programmers building mobile games should be familiar with the Unity and Marmalade mobile game engines, the two most popular engines for mobile. They should also be familiar with the iOS, Android, and Windows Phone platforms, for which the majority of mobile games are developed.

ROLES AND DUTIES

Because today's online games can be very complex, most programmers work in teams that focus on one aspect of game programming. The main roles are broken down as follows:

Online games require network programmers to manage multiplayer access and security. Here, a network programmer discusses new technologies with a network engineer.

The lead programmer is a seasoned programmer with solid experience in game development, and he or she is responsible for all programming concerns through the development lifecycle of a game. He or she supervises multiple teams of programmers and manages schedules and milestones. The role is as overseer, troubleshooter, and liaison with other teams working on the game.

The artificial intelligence programmer programs the computer-controlled characters and opponents, dictating how they react to the player's actions under various circumstances. The main concern is tuning behaviors to provide realism and a strategic challenge for the player.

The graphics programmer is an experienced programmer who understands everything about the needs of graphic artists, and he or she creates the tools artists use to create art assets and animation. He or she doesn't build the game so much as build tools that other programmers use to create 3-D and 2-D graphics that comprise the world, characters, objects, and effects in a game.

Online games require special programmers who manage multiplayer access and security over the Internet and cellular networks. The network programmer designs and implements pathways to the game so that many players can experience gameplay in real time. He or she is an expert at security, allowing users across the world to play without the threat of intrusion and cheating.

Every movement and motion in a game is controlled by lines of code. The physics programmer writes code that dictates natural laws of the world, for example, how long a character stays in the air when he jumps or how hard a race car slides when it hits an oil patch in *Need for Speed: Most Wanted* for the iPad and iPhone. Physics programmers touch everything that moves. There are even some who specialize in explosions and splashes.

Game code is structured in a way that segments are reused or repeated. The entire coding process goes much faster if machines do some of the work. The tools programmer writes code to automate some of the tasks required in game development. Examples are programs that convert or process art assets into a common format or generate tracks or paths.

The user interface (UI) programmer works closely with the game designers and artists to create and implement the

GAMING FACTS

- Forty-nine percent of U.S. households own at least one dedicated game console.
- The average game player age is thirty.
- Thirty-three percent of gamers play games on their smartphones.
- Forty-seven percent of puzzle, board, game show, trivia, and card games are played on mobile devices, the highest-rated category.
- Fifty-two percent of parents say video games are a positive part of their child's life.
- In the year of this writing, $24.75 billion were spent on games, hardware, and accessories in the United States.

menus game players use to navigate the game. These include settings menus and in-game menus, like weapon selection menus. The UI programmer also programs the button commands on console games, menus for online mobile games, and heads-up displays on flight simulators, first-person shooters, and other games that use them.

It's daunting to think that all of these programmatic elements can somehow come together and actually work, but they do. But successful game programmers, the ones that code the hit games, are able to take direction from designers and tune their work to make gameplay more compelling. As Bert Bingham, a producer at Gas Powered

ABOUT DEMOS

These days, all programmers breaking into the industry create demos, and most employers expect them. According to the Web site Education Portal, a good demo shows the prospective employer the applicant's proficiency with C++ and advanced algebra, skills used daily by programmers. Since the advent of mobile gaming platforms, programmers sometimes create demos in Flash, JavaScript, and other lighter languages. The originality of the demo concept is not as important as the execution. In other words, the demo should be clean and should work flawlessly, and the applicant should be able to explain the demo's workings in detail.

Games in Redmond, Washington, said in an interview published in *Occupational Outlook Quarterly*, "Almost any programmer can make a human player lose, but a truly good programmer knows how to make a player barely win."

EDUCATION

A programmer's job is highly technical, so a formal education is essential for programmers in the game industry. Naturally, success at high-level math and science courses lays the groundwork for advanced mathematics and computer science. Because technologies evolve and change rapidly, a programmer needs a firm foundation in the basics of computer languages in order to be able to rapidly learn new technologies as they emerge.

Most game programmers begin their careers in junior programmer positions, sometimes working for multiple teams, gaining experience in multiple specialty areas, such as those listed earlier in this section. As they gain experience, programmers may move into lead programmer positions. Lead programmers are required to have additional skills outside of their technical prowess, such as excellent leadership, communication, and management skills.

HIGH SCHOOL

High school students considering careers as programmers in the game industry should prepare for college by taking high-level courses in mathematics and the sciences. It is very important that students develop a firm foundation in algebra, calculus, and physics. More and more high schools are offering computer programming courses, and students should take advantage not only of these courses but also of the teacher resources. Students who begin to work in teams to make game demos will develop a lot of real-world skills and begin to build a portfolio of work they can use to demonstrate their skills and dedication when they apply to colleges or to companies offering internships.

POSTSECONDARY

Programming positions in the computer game industry are competitive. Applicants with the most impressive credentials and interpersonal skills have a big advantage. So while computing courses at technical and community colleges may be enough to gain a candidate a position at a second- or third-tier game developer, the best jobs are going to candidates with degrees in computer science or computer engineering from very good to excellent colleges and universities.

All programmers in the game industry will need expertise in a variety of computer languages, operating systems, and database analysis—especially C++, 3-D modeling, basic physics, and software engineering. Many will need to have a thorough knowledge of high-level math, especially vector graphics. Network programmers need to develop a knowledge of server security issues and resolutions. UI

The more established online game developers, such as EA Games, offer a variety of internships for high school and college students.

programmers usually have training in art. Many programmers at the best game companies have earned a master's degree in information systems, computer science, or mathematics. Programmers who hope to one day take positions as leads will benefit from business courses in management.

INTERNSHIPS AND TRAINING PROGRAMS

Because the programming field is so competitive among game companies, it is almost necessary for a student or graduate seeking a position to complete an internship. Applicants are expected to have excellent programming skills and a thorough understanding of the game development process. Interns may work on the user interface, or they may work on gameplay. Usually candidates must be able to program and debug in C++ and have specialty knowledge or expertise in one of the areas listed earlier in this section.

Most well-established publishers and studios are eager to hire qualified interns as programmers. Game giant Electronic Arts is known as having one of the best internship programs in the industry. Blizzard, Microsoft, Sony, and Zynga are just a few of the companies that offer programming internships.

CHAPTER 7

Tester, Quality Assurance, and Other Jobs

Testing is the process by which glitches in a game are discovered while the game is being developed. Quality assurance (QA) is a phase of testing that occurs in the postproduction phase—after all of the elements of the game are in place—and serves as a final quality check.

A tester's job is to find and document problems with the software: bugs, gameplay inconsistencies, and—in the early phases of a product's development cycle— design flaws. The job demands a high level of concentration, acute attention to detail, and excellent communication skills. As a game's ship date nears, testers work long hours under stressful conditions, and burnout is common. But for individuals who are determined to break into the game industry, the sacrifice is worth it.

In an interview with G4TV, Jeff Roper, a veteran QA project lead, spoke frankly about the challenges of the job: "Testing is hard work and can often be tedious. Someone who expects to just play video games all day will be disappointed. Someone who realizes that testing is a serious job, with high expectations, will be much more successful."

The requirements for a job as a tester are fairly broad in comparison to those for other roles. "The basic characteristics managers look for would be a fundamental love and passion for video games," Roper said. "Other important characteristics would be an eye for detail, critical thinking, and the ability to stay focused throughout. Of course, being a team player and getting along with your fellow coworkers is also important."

Testers using the role as a launching point for other jobs in the industry must demonstrate they can play games, have great attention to detail, and can communicate well with the team.

DUTIES

A tester's specific duties depend on the role he or she is assigned. The lead tester oversees the testing and reporting process. He or she is an experienced game tester who has demonstrated superlative leadership and organizational skills. The number-one responsibility is to organize and guide the team of testers. The lead tester also works with the producer and game designers to generate and implement test plans.

The lead tester is usually responsible for managing the bug database and the bug reporting system, hiring and training junior testers, and generally making sure things run smoothly and on time. Finally, the lead tester is a representative of the testing department, acting as a liaison between it and the broader development team, the publisher, and management.

The game tester plays one or more parts of a game again and again looking for issues. These could be issues with features working properly, gameplay balance, and crashes. Testers employ testing methodologies that are essentially routines used over and over again. This helps them isolate issues and replicate them so that they or the programmers can determine the issue's cause. Testers then document their findings and submit them to the design or production team, or to the lead tester.

EDUCATION REQUIREMENTS

To become a game tester, a college degree isn't always necessary. However, because these jobs are highly competitive, applicants with degrees will usually get preference. As with other roles, game companies look for people with a high interest level in games and a broad background that combines technical courses and liberal arts courses. Individuals without a formal post–high school education can sometimes break into the business with short-term contract positions that pay by the hour. In general, employers look for candidates who are methodical, have an above-average attention to detail, and possess excellent written and verbal communication skills.

HIGH SCHOOL

Ideally, a high school student who plans to start his or her career as a tester should take as many computer and math classes as possible. High-level English courses will also help prepare the student for report writing and verbal communication. Students should consider writing for the school newspaper or working on the yearbook or other student publications.

POSTSECONDARY

For a role as a tester, any postsecondary education helps. While college is the best option, graduates of community colleges and technical schools have a leg up on applicants

Working for your school yearbook can be an excellent way to gain experience with written and verbal communication, skills that are essential for working in a team environment.

with only high school diplomas. The most successful candidates have a bachelor's degree in computer science or computer engineering. They know the computing language C++, as well as scripting languages that are used for the automation of test cases. Another key area of study is communications. This can come in the form of technical writing, journalism, and even creative writing—all of which expose the student to the core concepts of clear thinking and efficient expression. Students who opt for technical school should have the opportunity to learn programming and scripting languages as well as technical writing. Any

Online social gaming is the fastest-growing segment within the video and computer game industry. There are plenty of opportunities for game testers in this segment of the market.

student who wishes to be a lead tester will benefit from management courses in the business school.

INTERNSHIPS AND TRAINING PROGRAMS

There are plenty of opportunities for testing internships, more so than for any other role in game development. Most larger publishers and studios offer summer internships, and many people who get jobs as testers get their start as interns. The best place to learn about available internships is on a game company's career portal or job board.

MORE JOBS IN ONLINE GAMES

The computer gaming industry, including companies that make games for online distribution, offers career opportunities for individuals who are passionate about games but who have interests outside of computer science. Those described here are perfect for people whose focus leans toward music, writing, or marketing and sales.

AUDIO ENGINEER

Audio engineers in the games industry make all the sounds in a game. They compose the background music and give voice to a game's characters. They also create every single incidental sound, such as explosions, splashes, plops, and crowd noise, just to name a few. They work closely with the game designers and artists to gain an understanding of the game objectives, character profiles, and worlds that make up the game. They also work with programmers on the process of incorporating the sounds into the game.

This position is well suited to individuals with strong backgrounds in both music and audio production. Game companies prefer a candidate with a bachelor's degree in music and technology or a degree in either music theory or sound engineering, and experience in audio production. Applicants usually take courses in computer science and engineering, sound recording, audio and music production, and music theory. Applicants with associate's degrees may also find junior-level positions at game companies and work their way through the ranks while learning on the job.

WRITER

Studios that make story-driven games often hire writers on their staffs or on a project basis. The writer may be tasked with working with the game designer to develop or polish threads in the story line or character dialogue. Writers may work on treatments, prototypes, and storyboards that help move the creative team in the right direction. Sometimes writers write strategy guides, user manuals, and other add-ons.

People who want to work as writers in the computer game industry must have excellent written and oral communication skills, understand conventional plot structures, and be fluid in the concepts associated with multi-thread plot structures. The writer must be able to work well in teams and be comfortable having his or her work picked apart by others. A strong foundation in grammar is also necessary. Writers typically earn bachelor's degrees in

AN INTERVIEW WITH DEREK DONAHUE, ASSISTANT PRODUCER INTERN, VISUAL CONCEPTS

Describe your job in five words.

Derek Donahue: I do all sorts of things. Mostly animation work, but I mess with code, do some QA work, and even gather references. I also do programming, play-testing, and motion capture.

What was the first game you ever played?

DD: I'm not exactly sure what the first game I ever played was, but I know my first console was the Nintendo 64, and I played a lot of *Mario Kart* and *Super Mario 64*. I also loved Pokemon Red and Blue on the Game Boy Color.

At what age did you first realize making games was what you wanted to do?

DD: Around seventh grade.

How did you become an intern?

DD: A game artist from 2K came to my high school's career day, and I told her about my interest in video game design. She got me in contact with a producer working on *MLB 2K10*, and after a couple of interviews, I was given a contract.

What advice would you give people who are seeking internships in the game industry?

DD: Make something. There are so many awesome tools out there for independent developers (Unity and Blender come to mind), and with enough practice, anyone can make something cool. When you show potential employers your work, they can see your creativity and that you are serious about pursuing a career in the industry.

INTERNSHIPS AND TRAINING PROGRAMS

Now that the online gaming industry is well established, more internships are available for university students. Some game companies are affiliated with design schools and use these relationships to hand-pick the most promising students to participate in internships. A student who succeeds at an internship is very likely to be offered a position with the company upon graduation. A game company prefers to hire someone who has proven he or she meets its standards and fits in well with its mission and vision. Internships are a great way to get a foot in the door.

A couple of companies that offer internships are Microsoft and Blizzard Entertainment. Microsoft, in its careers department, looks for qualifications such as pursuing a bachelor of arts degree in game design or its equivalent; a strong portfolio that demonstrates design fundamentals, techniques, storytelling, and game designs; strong knowledge of the tools used to create materials, such as Unreal, Unity, and Sketchup; a strong desire to work in teams and meet deadlines while learning new skills; and an ability to communicate vision to team members.

Blizzard Entertainment, located in Irvine, California, allows interns to work directly with development teams and business operations departments. Applicants must be studying at a university or college in the United States and be returning to school in the fall after the internship. The length of the internship is twelve weeks, paid, and offers opportunities during the summer months.

English, creative writing, or other writing-intensive liberal arts courses of study.

MARKETING AND SALES

It's one thing to make the games. But someone has to generate consumer interest and actually sell the games. Marketing and sales takes care of the business side of the computer game industry. Usually the smaller studios don't have much to offer for the entry-level applicant in this area; instead, the jobs are available at the big publishers like Sony, Electronic Arts, and Ubisoft, to name a few.

The marketing manager oversees all marketing and marketing materials related to a game. He or she creates a strategy by which the game will be marketed to the public, including Web presence, press releases, promo, print and TV ads, and cross-marketing.

The brand director is an upper-level job, responsible for the overall brand strategies for a development group within a publisher.

The market research analyst is a data cruncher who does the research and reports on what kinds of products will be successful, pricing structure, and where to sell the game.

The sales representative sells the game to wholesalers or retailers.

Creative services specialists create marketing materials such as boxes, manuals, CD case liners, and print promotional materials.

The best candidates for jobs in marketing and sales have bachelor's degrees and MBAs in marketing or business

Companies spend millions on attending trade shows and conferences to show off their latest products.

administration and a keen interest in the video game market. They will have worked in the industry in some capacity, possibly as a salesclerk at a video game retailer while in high school or college, as an intern at a game publisher, or as an aide at a large video game conference like the Game Developers Conference or E3.

Creative services teams are staffed with graphic artists and copywriters who can take direction from marketing and generate compelling packaging and marketing materials. They may have been trained in college, in art school, or at a trade school, usually in art or advertising.

aesthetic Having to do with a sense of the beautiful or pleasing.

bug A defect in a computer program.

C++ A commonly used object-oriented programming language.

crash A sudden failure of a computer program or system.

development cycle The entire process of creating a game.

documentation Manuals, listings, diagrams, and other written or graphic materials that describe the use, operation, maintenance, or design of a game.

Flash A multimedia platform used to add animation, video, and interactivity to a game.

imperative Absolutely necessary, required, or unavoidable.

integration The act of combining two or more things into a whole.

internship A position at an employer during which a novice acquires experience in that employer's industry.

iteration A repetition of one or more statements in a computer program.

Javascript A popular prototype-based scripting language used to create games for mobile phones.

liberal arts The academic course of instruction at a college intended to provide general knowledge and comprising the arts, humanities, natural sciences, and social sciences, as opposed to technical subjects.

portfolio A collection of samples that represent an individual's skills and talent.

prototype A model on which something is based.

software architecture A set of structures composed of software elements and their relationships with one another.

sublime Elevated or lofty in thought; supreme and outstanding.

3-D modeling A process by which a three-dimensional wireframe model is created using software.

tune To improve by making fine adjustments.

vector graphics Points, lines, curves, and polygons, based on mathematical expressions, that represent images in computer graphics.

vision A vivid, imaginative conception.

Entertainment Software Association (ESA)
575 7th Street NW
Washington, DC 20004
(202) 223-240
Web site: http://www.theesa.com
The Entertainment Software Association is exclusively
    dedicated to serving the business and public affairs
    needs of companies that publish computer and video
    games for video game consoles, personal computers,
    and the Internet.

Game Developer Magazine
600 Harrison Street, 6th Floor
San Francisco, CA 94107
(415) 947-6223
Web site: http://www.gdmag.com
This monthly publication delivers technical how-to
    articles to professionals creating hits for the PC,
    console, and arcade.

Graphic Artists Guild
32 Broadway, Suite 1114
New York, NY 10004
(212) 791-3400
Web site: http://www.graphicartistsguild.org
The guild promotes and protects the social, economic,
    and professional interests of animators, cartoonists,
    designers, illustrators, and digital artists at all skill levels.

International Game Developers Association (IGDA)
19 Mantua Road
Mt. Royal, NJ 08061
(856) 423-2990
Web site: http://www.igda.org
This is the largest nonprofit membership organization
   serving individuals who create video games.

WEB SITES

Due to the changing nature of Internet links, Rosen Publishing has developed an online list of Web sites related to the subject of this book. This site is updated regularly. Please use this link to access the list:

http://www.rosenlinks.com/CICT/Game

Brathwaite, Brenda. *Breaking Into the Game Industry: Advice for a Successful Career from Those Who Have Done It*. Boston, MA: Cengage Learning, 2012.

Dille, Flint, and John Zuur Platten. *The Ultimate Guide to Video Game Writing and Design*. Los Angeles, CA: Lone Eagle, 2008.

Eddy, Brian. *Classic Video Games: The Golden Age, 1971– 1884*. Oxford, England: Shire, 2012.

Habgood, Jacob, and Mark Overmars. *The Game Maker's Apprentice: Game Development for Beginners*. New York, NY: Apress, 2006.

Hodgson, David, and Bryan Stratton. *Video Game Careers*. Roseville, CA: Prima Games, 2008.

Marx, Christy. *Write Your Way into Animation and Games*. Burlington, MA: Focal Press, 2010.

Melissinos, Chris, and Patrick O'Rourke. *The Art of Video Games: From Pac-Man to Mass Effect*. New York, NY: Welcome Books, 2012.

Moore, Michael. *Introduction to the Game Industry*. Upper Saddle River, NJ: Prentice Hall, 2006.

Mott, Tony, and Peter Molyneux. *1001 Video Games You Must Play Before You Die*. New York, NY: Universe Publishing, 2010.

Novak, Jeannie. *Game Development Essentials: An Introduction*. Independence, KY: Delmar Cengage Learning, 2007.

Patterson, James, and Ned Rust. *Daniel X: Game Over.* New York, NY: Little, Brown and Company, 2011.

Rogers, Scott. *Level Up: The Guide to Great Video Game Design.* West Sussex, England: John Wiley & Sons, 2010.

Sailors, John. *Flying the Coop: The Video Game Mystery Novel.* Livermore, CA: Story Crest, 2012.

Sterling, Dackeyia. *How to Find Video Game Internships: Premium Contacts & Strategies for Launching Your Video Game Career.* Bowie, MD: Key Quest, 2012.

Adams, Ernest. *Break Into the Game Industry.* Emeryville, CA: McGraw-Hill/Osborne, 2003.

Blizzard Entertainment. "Internship Program." Retrieved August 16, 2012 (http://us.blizzard .com/en-us/company/careers/university-relations/ internships.html).

Brockman, Joshua. "When Play Means Pay: Video Game Jobs on the Rise." National Public Radio. Retrieved August 3, 2012 (http://www.npr.org/templates/story/story.php? storyId=122290666).

Christian Science Monitor. "Video Game Nation: Why So Many Play." Retrieved July 1, 2012 (http://www.csmonitor.com/ USA/Society/2012/0318/Video-game-nation-Why-so -many-play).

Digipen. "BS in Computer Engineering." Retrieved July 28, 2012 (https://www.digipen.edu/?id=1265).

Digipen. "BS in Computer Science in Game Design." Retrieved July 28, 2012 (https://www.digipen.edu/academics/ degree-programs/bs-in-game-design).

Digipen. "BS in Computer Science in Real-Time Interactive Simulation." Retrieved July 28, 2012 (https://www.digipen .edu/academics/degree-programs/real-time-interactive -simulation).

Digipen. "BS in Engineering Sound Design." Retrieved July 28, 2012 (https://www.digipen.edu/?id=9353).

Digipen. "BA in Music and Sound Design." Retrieved July 28, 2012 (https://www.digipen.edu/academics/degree -programs/bamsd).

A Digital Dreamer. "How to Become a Video Game Designer, and What It Takes to Do Well in Video Game Design." Retrieved August 1, 2012 (http://www.adigitaldreamer .com/articles/becomeavideogamedesigner.htm).

A Digital Dreamer. "Video Game Art Careers." Retrieved August 17, 2012 (http://www.adigitaldreamer.com/articles /video-game-art.htm).

Duffy, Jill. "Ask the Experts. 'How to Become a Producer.'" Retrieved August 12, 2012 (http://www .gamecareerguide.com/news/12135/ask_the_experts_ how_to_become_a_.php).

Education Portal. "Gaming Engineer: Salary and Career Information." Retrieved July 1, 2012 (http://education -portal.com/articles/Gaming_Engineer_Salary_and_ Career_Information.html).

Entertainment Software Association. "Essential Facts About the Computer and Video Game Industry: Sales, Demographic and Usage Data." Retrieved July 2, 2012 (https://www .theesa.com).

Entertainment Software Association. "Games: Improving the Economy." Retrieved July 16, 2012 (http://www.theesa.com /games-improving-what-matters/economy.asp).

Gamespot. "So You Wanna Be a Game Designer." Retrieved July 19, 2012 (http://www.gamespot.com/features/so-you -wanna-be-a-game-designer-6129276/?page=2).

Guadiosi, John. "New Reports Forecast Global Video Game Industry Will Reach $82 Billion by 2017." Retrieved July 1, 2012 (http://www.forbes.com/sites/johngaudiosi/2012/07 /18/new-reports-forecasts-global-video-game-industry-will -reach-82-billion-by-2017).

Hodgson, David, and Bryan Stratton. *Paid to Play: An Insider's Guide to Video Game Careers.* Roseville, CA: Prima Games, 2006.

Hodgson, David, and Bryan Stratton. *Video Game Careers.* Roseville, CA: Prima Games, 2008.

Lehrman, Robert. "The Video Game Revolution." History of Gaming. Retrieved July 2, 2012 (http://www.pbs.org/kcts/videogamerevolution/history).

Media Arts. "Game Art & Design." Retrieved August 12, 2012 (http://www.artinstitutes.edu/pittsburgh/media-arts/game-art-and-design-bs-4112.aspx).

Newan, Ryan, and Brandon Sheffield. "Game Developer Salary Survey 2011." Retrieved July 1, 2012 (http://www.gamecareerguide.com/features/980/game_developer_salary_survey_2011.php).

Occupational Outlook Quarterly. "Work for Play: Careers in Video Game Development." Retrieved July 13, 2012 (http://www.bls.gov/opub/ooq/2011/fall/art01.pdf).

OEDb. "The Ultimate Guide to Video Game Degrees and Careers." Retrieved June 22, 2012 (http://oedb.org/library/features/video-game-degrees-and-careers).

O-Net. "Summary Report for Multimedia Artists and Animators." Retrieved August 12, 2012 (http://www.onetonline.org/link/summary/27-1014.00).

Rollings, Andrew, and Ernest Adams. *Andrew Rollings and Ernest Adams on Game Design.* San Francisco, CA: New Riders Group, 2003.

Thang, Jimmy. "The Tough Life of a Games Tester." Retrieved August 2, 2012 (http://www.ign.com/articles/2012/03/29/the-tough-life-of-a-games-tester).

Zingtech. "Internships in the Game Industry." Retrieved August 16, 2012 (http://www.zingtech.com/features/gamedev/eainternship.htm).

Index

mobile games, most popular, 28
mobile gaming, 9–11, 12–13
modelers, 25
Multi-User Dungeon (MUD)
     games, 7
Myspace, 11

N

Nokia, 9

O

online gaming, history of, 7–8

P

producers
   duties, 32, 33–36
   education requirements,
     36–40
   internships and training
     programs, 40–41
programmers
   duties, 50–54
   education requirements,
     54–57
   internships and training
     programs, 57

Q

Quake, 7

S

Snake, 9
social gaming, 4, 11–12, 12–13

T

tester/quality assurance
   duties, 58, 59
   education requirements, 60–63
   internships and training
     programs, 63
Twitter, 11

U

Ultima Online, 7

W

World of Warcraft, 8, 10, 24
writers, 64–67

Z

Zynga, 11–12, 57

ABOUT THE AUTHOR

J. Poolos is the author of nonfiction books on a variety of topics, most recently *Designing, Building, and Maintaining Web Sites* in the Digital and Information Literacy series. He spent twelve years as a writer in the computer game industry.

PHOTO CREDITS